Hermie: A Common Caterpillar
is also available in board book, video, and DVD.

Based on the bestseller *Just Like Jesus* for adults.

A Just Like Jesus Story

HeRMIe
A Common Caterpillar

MAX LUCADO

Illustrations by GlueWorks Animation

Tommy NELSON®

www.tommynelson.com

A Division of Thomas Nelson, Inc.
www.ThomasNelson.com

Text and art copyright © 2002 by Max Lucado.
Illustrations by GlueWorks Animation.

Karen Hill, Administrative Editor for Max Lucado.

Published in Nashville, Tennessee, by Tommy Nelson®, a Division of Thomas Nelson, Inc.

Library of Congress Cataloging-in-Publication Data

Lucado, Max.
    Hermie: a common caterpillar / Max Lucado.
        p. cm.
    "A just like Jesus story."
    Summary: Best friends Hermie and Wormie are sad each time they see that other creatures are special
when they, themselves, are so ordinary, but they trust that they are *special* in God's eyes and that He is not
finished with them yet.
    ISBN 1-4003-0117-3
    [1. Caterpillars—Fiction. 2. Self-esteem—Fiction. 3. Christian life—Fiction 4. Friendship—Fiction.
5. Metamorphosis—Fiction.] I. Title.

P27.L9684 He 2002
[Fic]—dc21   2002026439

Printed in the United States of America
02 03 04 05 WRZ 5 4 3 2 1

To Jan Karney, Kendra Kunkel, and the
Oak Hills Church of Christ nursery workers.
Thank you for loving our babies.

"Wow!" said Hermie the caterpillar as he tilted his head and looked at the tree above him.

A beautiful butterfly was resting on a large green leaf. His brightly colored wings were covered with dazzling white spots.

Hermie held his breath and whispered to himself, "He's about to fly." And with a lift of his wings, he was in the air, circling softly in the summer sky.

"Oh, how I'd love to fly like that," Hermie wished.

He watched until the butterfly was a speck in the sky. Then Hermie sighed and turned away.

Now, as a rule, caterpillars aren't very exciting. But Hermie was even more ordinary than most.

Some caterpillars have spots. Not Hermie.

Some caterpillars have stripes. Not Hermie.

He had nothing but smooth green skin and a bunch of feet. Hermie was a common caterpillar.

Hermie ate common leaves . . . squirmed through common grass . . . did common stuff. Hermie was a common caterpillar.

Hermie did one thing, however, that was uncommon.
He talked to God. He talked to God about all sorts of things.
And God would talk back to Hermie. Of course, he didn't
really hear God out loud. God spoke to his heart.

Late at night when the other caterpillars were asleep,
Hermie would crawl out from his bed and stare at the sky
and talk to God.

"God, why did You make me so common? Other caterpillars
have stripes. Some have spots. I even saw one with spots and
stripes. But me? I don't have anything. I'm just . . . Hermie."

"And I'm just Wormie," said a nearby voice.

Hermie turned and saw a caterpillar that looked like him. No spots. No stripes. Another common caterpillar, his friend Wormie.

Once Hermie had told the other caterpillars that he talked to God—and they laughed. But not Wormie. He understood. That's how they had become friends. Wormie talked to God, too.

When Hermie and Wormie felt common, God would tell them, "Don't worry. I love you both just the way you are, but I'm not finished with you yet."

And so they would feel better . . . for a while. But then something else would happen and they would feel common again. Like the day they met an ant. The ant was smaller than either of them, but on his shoulder was a big pine cone. They were amazed at the strength of the ant.

"My!" Wormie exclaimed. "How do you carry such a big load?"

"It's how God made me. He made me strong."

And off marched the tiny ant with the big load.

That night Hermie and Wormie asked God, "Why can't we be strong like the ant? We could never do what he could. Why did You make us so common?"

God's answer was the same as always. "Don't worry, Hermie and Wormie. I'm not finished with you yet. I'm giving you a heart like Mine."

And they felt better, at least until they saw a snail.

One afternoon, the sky opened up and the rain drenched the ground.
The two friends hurried as fast as they could to find a dry place.
Suddenly, they heard a low, scratchy voice.

"Looks like you're in a hurry."

Hermie and Wormie stopped. They looked all around but saw no
one. "Did you hear something?" Hermie asked.

"I did," Wormie replied. That's when Hermie saw the head of a snail
peeking out of his shell. "Look, Wormie, over there by that rock."

"Greetings," said the snail. "Looks like you're trying to get out of the rain."

"We surely are," Hermie answered. "We're getting soaked."

"You need a house like I have," said the snail.

"That's your house?" Wormie asked.

"It sure is. Watch." And with that . . .

. . . the snail pulled his head into his shell.

"See, it's nice and dry in here. I take my house with me everywhere I go," his voice echoed.

The two friends were discouraged. They wondered why God hadn't given them a neat house like the snail's.

Later that night, when the rain had passed and everyone else was asleep, Hermie and Wormie asked God why He gave the snail such a neat house and them nothing at all. "Why do we have to be so common?" they wanted to know.

Again, God's answer was kind and patient. "Don't worry, Hermie. Don't worry, Wormie. I love you both. And I'm not finished with you yet."

So they felt better. And for a long time, just thinking about how much God loved them made Hermie and Wormie feel special, and not so common, until . . .

. . . one day they saw a ladybug. Oh, what beautiful black
spots she had! Neither of the caterpillars had ever seen
such perfect spots. Jet black and exact circles.

"You have such pretty spots!" Hermie exclaimed.

"Gorgeous!" Wormie agreed.

"Oh, thank you," she answered softly. Then the ladybug
blushed, because she was very shy.

"I mean it," Wormie continued. "We've never seen anyone with such beautiful spots."

"You are very kind," she replied. "But I had nothing to do with it. This is the way God made me."

Hermie and Wormie wanted to be grateful for the gift God had given the ladybug, but it was hard. Both of them felt so . . . common.

That night, underneath the bright stars, Hermie prayed. "God, we know You are good and wise. We know You love us just as we are. But we don't understand why You made us like this. We're so very . . ."

"Common?" God finished the sentence.

"Yes, common," both caterpillars said at the same time.

"Remember," God told them. "I love you just the way you are, but I'm not finished with you yet. I'm giving you a heart like Mine."

Hermie sighed. He wanted to feel better. He tried to feel better. Usually, he did feel better. But that night he still felt sad. He also felt tired. Very tired. More tired than usual.

Wormie," he told his friend, "I'm so very sleepy.
I feel like I need to sleep a long time."

"Then let's make you a soft, comfy bed."
It took them awhile to find just the right leaf.

"There," Wormie said to his friend. "Have a good, long rest. I'll be waiting for you when you wake up."

Hermie thanked his friend. Then he prayed to God and said, "You know, God, it's okay that I'm just a common caterpillar. You love me, and *that* makes me special."

Hermie snuggled into his bed, closed his eyes, and drifted off to sleep.

As he slept, he dreamed that he was different.

He had strength like the ant.

He had a house like the snail.

He had spots like the ladybug.

He dreamed that he was no longer a common caterpillar but that he had something special.

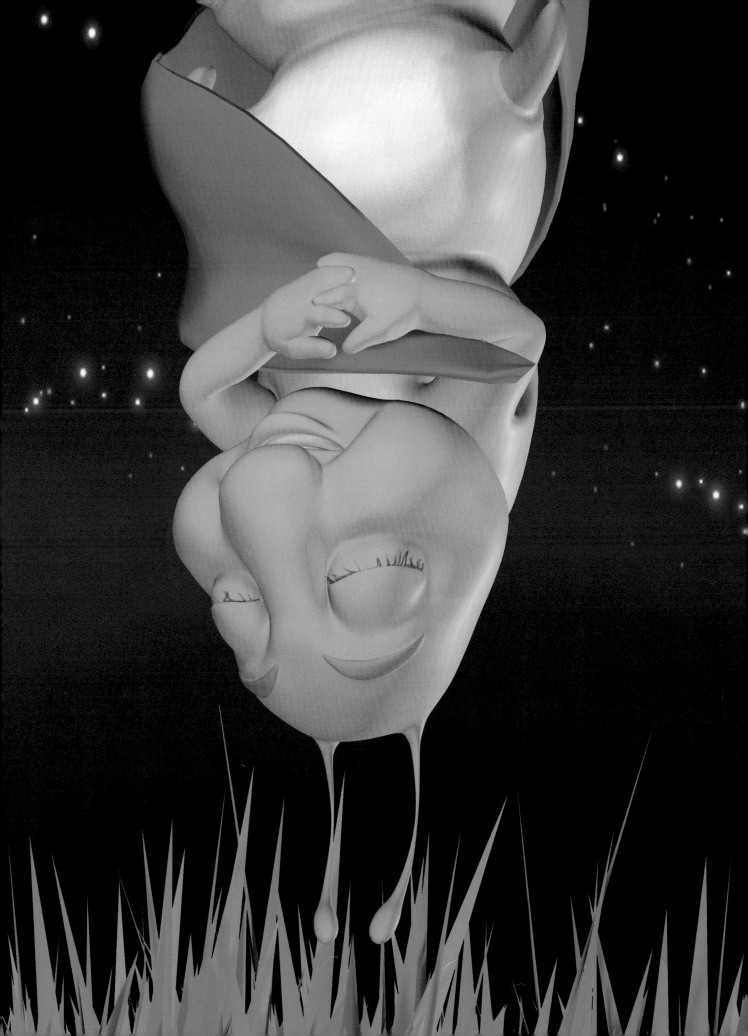

After what seemed to be a long time, he woke up. He thought he had slept through the day and into the night because everything around him was dark.

He was covered from head to toe. What had happened to his comfy bed? He wiggled and squirmed to get out, and when he did . . .

. . . he and his bed began to fall.

Suddenly, his bed cracked open, and Hermie
felt a tickle on his back.

Something wonderful happened. . . .

Wings fluttered open! Wings he didn't even know he had.

They were glorious, wide, brightly colored wings with beautiful spots . . . and they were *his*.

With hardly any effort, Hermie began to fly. Up and up, higher and higher.

That's when Hermie realized what God had done. Now he understood.

God had made Hermie special—inside and out.

He wasn't like the ant . . . or the snail . . . or the ladybug.

He was unique!
   One of a kind!
      No one else was exactly like him.
         He was Hermie—a beautiful butterfly with a beautiful heart.

He soared high through the air, to the right and to the left. Then he thought of his friend Wormie. From the air Hermie looked down at his broken bed. Nearby were the ant, the snail, and the ladybug. They were all talking to Wormie.

As Hermie floated downward, he could hear Wormie saying, "I don't know what happened to Hermie. He was asleep in his special bed, and now I can't find him!"

"Wormie!" came a voice from high in the sky.

Wormie heard his friend's voice and was excited.

"Hermie, where are you?"

"I'm up here!"

Wormie looked up. "Hermie? Is that really you?"

"Yes, it's really me."

"Wow!" said the ant. "You look so different."

"Goodness!" gasped the snail. "You are so big."

"Gracious!" admired the ladybug. "You are the most beautiful butterfly I've ever seen."

"God was not finished with me after all!" Hermie announced. Then he flew down and stopped right next to Wormie.

He gave a big butterfly grin and whispered, "Wormie, God loves you just the way you are. But, guess what? God is not finished with you, either, my friend."

"You don't think so?"

"I know He's not."

"You know? You may be right. I'm starting to feel pretty sleepy, too." Wormie yawned a big yawn.

Hermie smiled a big smile.